TOP 10
QUICKBOOKS
SNAFUs
How to NOT be a NUB

By Dida Clifton

The Office Squad
7495 W. Azure Drive, Suite 110
Las Vegas, NV 89130
www.theofficesquad.com

©2020 TheOfficeSquad

Illustrations by Alex Raffi

Printed in the United States of America

ISBN 978-0-578-65384-6

This book and the company culture that created it would have never happened without the following:

My Mom and Dad for "suggesting" I join the military

My amazing husband, the fighter pilot, who supports all my endeavors (no matter how crazy) with minimal pushback

My loving, grown daughters who let me believe that I'm the perfect mom

My Squad for giving life to our company culture

Aim High,

Dida

TABLE OF CONTENTS

Preface 7

Introduction 9

Chapter 1 10
Top Priority Information: Your Chart of Accounts

Chapter 2 14
A Real Goat Rope: Ignoring Your Balance Sheet

Chapter 3 16
Review Your Numbers or Miss the Target

Chapter 4 18
An "ID 10 T" Problem: Mixing Business Funds & Personal Funds

Chapter 5 22
FUBAR-Proof Credit Card Tracking

Chapter 6 25
Entering a Bill but Not Paying It

Chapter 7 27
Receiving Payments for Duplicate Income

Chapter 8 32
Don't be the FNG: Vendors vs. Employees

Chapter 9 35
Check Your 6: Reconcile or Go Down in Flames

Chapter 10 37
Do the Impossible: Enter Every Damn Thing

The Gloss 39
Glossary of Jargon, Slang & Acronyms (QuickBooks & Air Force)

NATO Alphabet 45

Dida Clifton

PREFACE

There are a lot of books, classes, and consultants out there that will teach you bookkeeping and accounting. This is not one of them. This book is a guide to help self-taught, solo-flying QuickBooks users dodge the deadliest of mistakes. Deadly you say? Is it really that big of a deal? Roger that! I've seen the killer stress generated when tax time arrives or the IRS audits a business and the owners scramble to find someone who can rebuild years of bookkeeping. They scramble to find documents and data, not to mention the funds to pay for the work, all the while trying to continue to run their business. I see it firsthand and it isn't pretty.

This is no joke, newbie! I tell it to you straight so you don't spiral out of control. For more than two decades, business owners doing their own books have come to me for assistance. Time and time again they've made big mistakes in the same 10 areas. And what starts out as innocent errors, ignored entries, or rushed work soon becomes a real SNAFU. Before you know it, your books are FUBARed and your entire mission is compromised.

If this happens to you it's not the end of the world. There is help—after all, TheOfficeSquad does the impossible every day. But you won't need a massive rescue and a big sack of money if you take the time to brief yourself early and you ask for help from your Squad. If you're a QuickBooks veteran, consider this book your checklist; it's a true test and refresh of your solo-flying skills. Affirmative?

Dida Clifton
The OfficeSquad(R) Commander, CEO and Founder
F-15 Squadron Operations Specialist,
Holloman AFB, a long, long time ago.

Dida Clifton

INTRODUCTION

Civvy, I salute your resourcefulness. Whether you're selling virtual gadgets or servicing cloud-based contraptions, it's vital that you get all your accounting ducks in a row. This guide will give you necessary respect for QuickBooks, helping you complete your ongoing mission. It's short enough to be a reference, but long enough to cover some serious fundamentals. It's sure to help you commence if you're a total NUB, but it's also great intel for troubleshooting any QuickBooks mission in progress.

Initiate full-throttle!

Col. Q. Books
TheOfficeSquad Commander

p.s. Dida does solid work here, but I'll stand by and interject when you need to open your ears and look up for serious assistance.

TOP PRIORITY INFORMATION: YOUR CHART OF ACCOUNTS
(CHAPTER 1)

If you're an accounting veteran, this COA lesson isn't for you. But if you're here for Basic Training in the mission of bookkeeping, this intel is essential.

Accounts:
In bookkeeping, "accounts" doesn't just refer to actual bank accounts. Your "accounts" are numerous records that you set up to individually track resources, transactions, or events affecting your books. QuickBooks sets this up for you automatically when you "start a new company." The program will ask questions at setup about your company and create your COA based on your answers.

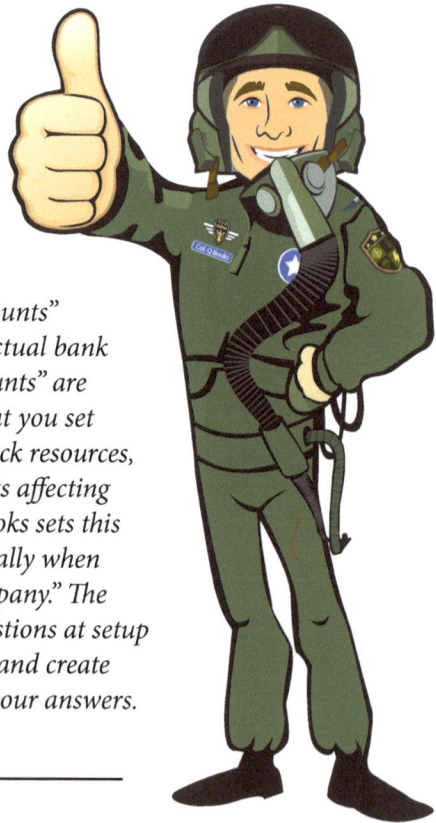

Dida Clifton

WHAT THE COA IS &
WHY IT COMMANDS RESPECT

Your Chart of Accounts, or COA for short, is the top dog; it's the first and most important section you'll set up in your QuickBooks. The COA lists each of your assets, liabilities, income, and expense accounts. Everything in QuickBooks connects to your COA and operations flow through it with double entry accounting as you input each entry affecting your business' books. Every time you make an entry in your QuickBooks—be it a check, a debit card purchase, a credit card charge, a bill to a client, or a bill from a vendor—it all flies through your COA twice.

If you screw up the setup of your Chart of Accounts, you'll pay the price. The way you set it up determines which account your entries end up in, and affects what you will see in your QuickBooks-generated reports. If garbage goes into QuickBooks, garbage comes out in the form of incorrect reports.

The Ugly Truth: If you screw up the setup of your COA, your reports will be useless garbage.

ACCOUNT NAMES & NUMBERS

In the image above there is a small list of expense accounts, each with an identifying name and number next to it. For most small businesses, these numbers aren't really necessary. When you set up the names of each of your accounts, fancy and frilly names just won't fly. Use descriptive account names that are easy for you and your accountant to understand and easy to find in the list. Look out for duplicates. Example: gas, fuel, and auto fuel are all the same thing. You only need one.

When you first set up your company's QuickBooks data file, the software will ask you to select your industry. QuickBooks then automatically sets up your COA based on your response, generating a simple list of the account types most commonly used in your industry. Review your COA and make sure you understand the title of each account in your income, expenses, assets, liability, and equity. You can add accounts and remove accounts (so long as nothing has been posted toward them) using the "edit" feature. Keep it simple and easy to read—The Taxman just needs accuracy. When you run financial reports, these accounts are what you'll see, and the numbers generated come from your input.

Dida Clifton

CHAOS WITH DEBITS AND CREDITS OR DOUBLE-ENTRY ACCOUNTING

Now that we've discussed the COA, account names, and numbers it's a good time to mention double-entry accounting. The double-entry accounting system recognizes that every transaction has two effects. For example, when you spend cash, you also gain something of value. And when you make sales, you also lose something of value.

Before accounting technologies like QuickBooks, these entries were done by hand on a giant green paper ledger. You'd post journal entries in the general ledger making sure you entered a debit in the correct column and the credit in the correct column, manually adding all of it together to create your reports.

QuickBooks makes it easy and does both of those entries for you. For example, you enter your transaction as a check as in the graphic below. The "bank account" window is the account from your COA that is debited. The expense window at the bottom left is where you choose the account for your credit. These accounts are all from your Chart of Accounts. If you're doing things wrong here, it all flows to your reports, which QuickBooks calculates for you.

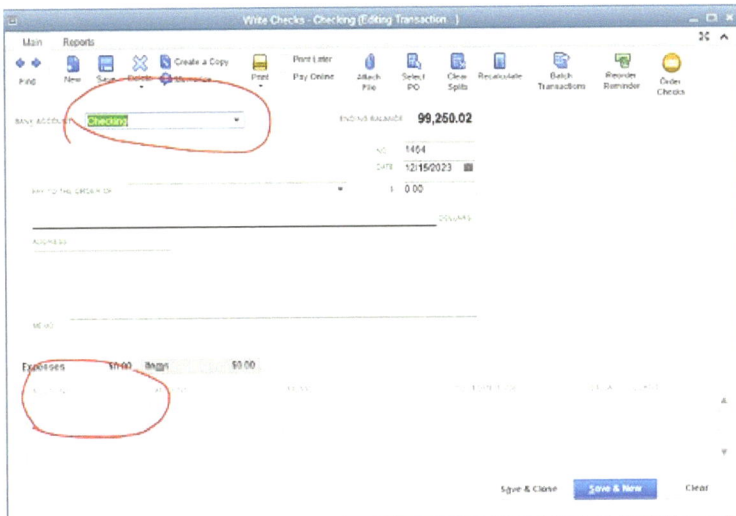

A REAL GOAT ROPE: IGNORING YOUR BALANCE SHEET
(CHAPTER 2)

Can your business continue to fund its own ascent? The Profit and Loss Statement (P&L), (a.k.a. the Revenue/Income Statement), is the financial report that gets the most publicity. But it's only half the picture! Don't look only at your Profit & Loss Statement; together with your Balance Sheet you'll find the answers to *where have I been, how am I doing, and where am I going.*

You don't have to be a Top Gun to get this; any Pop Tart can make this cut. Just remember this:

> *Balance Sheet = Summary of your company's financial health*

> *+ Profit & Loss Statement = Report of your sales and expenses*

> *Viewed every month, together, these show how your business is TRULY doing*

The main formula behind the Balance Sheet is this: Assets = Liabilities + Shareholders' Equity. This means that assets, or the means used to operate the company, are balanced by a company's financial obligations along with the equity investment brought into the company and its retained earnings. The total assets must equal the liabilities, plus the equity of the company.

Dida Clifton

So what does this mean? I have no idea. Ask an accountant. What I do know is...

Assets are the cash in the company, any property you can sell for cash, any loans you can collect on, and/or any customer invoices, a.k.a. Accounts Receivable, that you expect to collect.

Liabilities are the credit card balances you owe, any loans you're paying back, and bills you need to pay (a.k.a. Accounts Payable).

Equity is the funds you and any partners have put into the company. And if you put cash in the company, you can take it out without a tax issue.

Let's say you're a small business owner and you're not taking a salary. No paycheck. Sound familiar? Most likely you're taking draws straight from your equity. The money subtracted when you take a draw is not reported on the Profit and Loss. That account is on the Balance Sheet. It's an equity account. So if you're looking at your P&L, it shows a profit, and you're scratching your head thinking, "That can't be right? Where's all the money? It's not in my bank account."

It's on the balance sheet. Your equity draws, your loan payments, your credit card payments, and so on. They are all shown on the Balance Sheet. They are not income or expenses, which show on your Profit and Loss (P&L) report. They are assets and liabilities that show on your Balance Sheet. Copy that?

When small business owners need a wingman, they outsource their bookkeeping to TheOfficeSquad. When we assess the situation, we often find that the P&L is the only part of their QuickBooks that was being viewed regularly. The businesses are entering invoices to their clients in order to count revenue/income. They may even be entering expenses and reconciling the bank account. But way too often the Balance Sheet is totally ignored.

When preparing the end-of-year taxes, your accountant will need your correct balance sheet along with your interest paid, draws paid to the owner, and depreciation. If you or someone knowledgeable does your bookkeeping properly, preparing for taxes is blue skies.

REVIEW YOUR NUMBERS OR MISS THE TARGET
(CHAPTER 3)

Are you looking at the numbers? I mean really looking? I'm a business owner and bookkeeper, but I wasn't really looking at the numbers. Sure, I was looking at the checking account balance. I was also paying attention to the bills and to where the money seemed to be going.

Then I started working with a CFO who, fortunately, gave me a serious wakeup call by showing me the full picture. We studied the numbers from my Profit & Loss Report, the Balance Sheet, the Accounts Receivable Report, the Accounts Payable Report and the Cash Flow Report. When I viewed all these numbers together, it was the first time I'd seen where my business has been and where it was heading. Wow. Talk about a reality check!

> *Look at ALL your important numbers on a regular basis – that's the ONLY way to check your 6 AND your 12! And if you don't know how to read the reports, there's no excuse; you need to learn. Your future success depends on it. No Sh!t.*

Dida Clifton

I was lucky—the reality of my numbers that day was all about growth. But what if your numbers are headed in the wrong direction? If you're looking at the full picture on a monthly basis, you can catch negative trends early and change your flight path.

If you've outsourced your bookkeeping, that's great! It's a major step in growing your business. Make sure that your bookkeeper shares complete financials with you every month. Not every quarter, not twice a year, not annually—you need to see them every single month. When you ask for the reports and your bookkeeper waffles, that's a serious red flag—something's wrong. They are too busy for their workload or worse. Fraud happens when you're not paying attention. Studies show that 77% of occupational frauds were committed by someone working in accounting and operations.

Civvy, don't be a NUB.
Use QuickBooks correctly so your
reports are up-to-date AND easy to
access. Then look at them regularly.

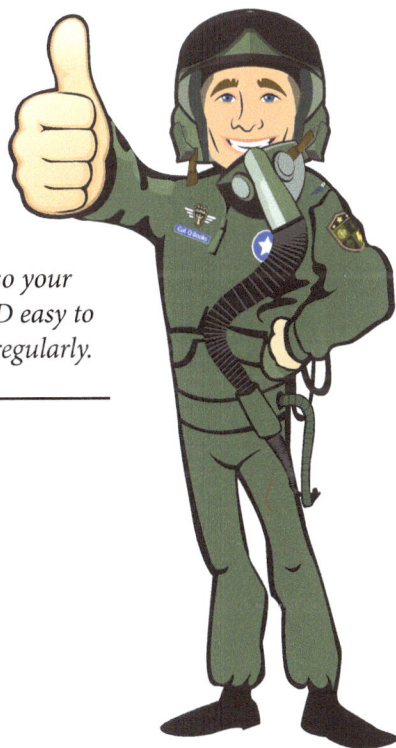

AN "ID 10 T" PROBLEM: MIXING BUSINESS FUNDS & PERSONAL FUNDS
(CHAPTER 4)

Many owners of small businesses fund their business using personal money or personal credit cards. Or they pay their personal bills using money from the business. This is because most beginner-level business owners don't "pay" themselves as they would an employee. This makes it difficult for anyone reviewing the books to draw a line where the owner's personal finances end and where the business' finances begin—it's really blurry. This is no problem if the bookkeeping is done correctly, but too often it's not. Let's take a look at where (and how) this can scramble signals in your books.

> *Business Funds*
> *+ Personal Funds*
> *x Mixed Up in QuickBooks*
> *= The Danger Zone!*

Dida Clifton

SCENARIO 1:

You need to pay your mortgage but your personal account doesn't have the funds. The business account does. It's okay to use the money from your business (assuming it's all yours and not your wingman's), as long as you understand how to post it correctly in your accounting software.

DON'T:

Write checks directly from your business account for personal bills. This means zero direct ACH payments or direct debit card payments for your home mortgage (or rent), nor for your personal car payment, nor for your personal credit card payments.

DO:

If you are paying your personal bills using funds from your business, you should write yourself a check from your business or transfer business funds to your personal account. This is a credit from your business checking account and a debit to your equity account (owner draw). Then pay the bills from that personal account.

Any checks you write to yourself are posted toward an owner's equity account, so the transaction shows on your balance sheet. This keeps personal items from showing up as expenses on your business' financial reports

Reality Check: You'll wait until the last minute to pay that mortgage payment so writing a check, depositing it to personal, writing another check, and mailing it won't happen. Who has time for that? What will really happen is you'll pay your mortgage online using the business bank account. When you do, post the transaction correctly in the business account as an owner's draw and note in the memo what you paid.

SCENARIO 2:

The business has an expense that the business account can't cover at the moment. You'll need to use your personal funds to pay for it.

DON'T:

Do not write a personal check made out to your business, and deposit and record it like you would a payment from your customers.

> **Reality Check:** *This will look like revenue on your Profit and Loss. You don't want to overstate your business revenue and pay taxes on your loans to the company.*

DO:

Deposit funds from your personal account to your business account and post the transaction in your QuickBooks as a loan from the owner. Then use those funds to pay the business expense.

Handling this correctly not only keeps you out of trouble for comingling funds, but it also ensures accurate financial reports.

Keep the blue side up!

Reality Check: *Here's what will really happen in this scenario. The business owner gets a call that an invoice is due for the business and the only funds available to pay it at the moment are his/her personal credit card or personal account debit card. So the vendor is paid over the phone or online using a personal account. How you post this transaction in your QuickBooks requires several entries.*

Dida Clifton

1. First, enter the business expense as a bill in QuickBooks.

2. Then you need to pay the bill in the software using funds from your equity or draw account. You'll probably need to use a "clearing account" or "petty cash" account to make that happen since the software won't allow you to pay things directly from an equity account.

3. In that same equity account, you'll post a loan from the owner.

FUBAR-PROOF CREDIT CARD TRACKING
(CHAPTER 5)

We're midflight, halfway to our destination. To grease your landing, you'll need to know that a common DIY QuickBooks error is not entering credit card transactions correctly. They are often not entered into the books at all, resulting in a lost opportunity for a tax deduction.

Don't let your tax deductions go MIA.

Dida Clifton

Let's revisit your Chart of Accounts. You'll remember it lists all of your business' accounts, including bank accounts, assets, and liabilities. Also listed are credit card accounts.

Adding your business' credit cards to QuickBooks is pretty straightforward. Set up a new account in the chart of accounts, and make sure to select "credit card" for the account type. You're now ready to enter your credit card transactions.

Each time you use that card for a purchase it needs to be entered in your bookkeeping and posted to the correct expense account. You can do this manually, or you have the option to download and sync your QuickBooks with the credit card company's records.

Just remember the download must then be reviewed for accuracy, and each transaction requires an "add" until you've mapped everything. Basically, the sync is not quite as easy as Intuit and the banks would like you to think. The items need to match exactly or the software doesn't recognize and match the transaction. This causes duplicates.

Monthly account reconciliations are vital to your flight plan.

Credit card accounts are just like your bank accounts when it comes to monthly statements and reconciling. Don't forget to reconcile. Each credit card account needs to be reconciled every single month. If you carry a balance on those cards, that balance shows up on your balance sheet as a liability. The payments you make on those cards post to the liability account and reduce the amount of your debt. Keeping all these things entered correctly, reconciled, and current creates accurate numbers.

> **Reality Check:** *Accurate and reconciled bookkeeping is the solid foundation for understanding your business' finances. If you don't take the time to do it or have it done, you're flying blind.*

ENTERING A BILL BUT NOT PAYING IT
(CHAPTER 6)

Common mistake number six is a SNAFU-interceptor focused on your Bill Pay module, which is a part of your Accounts Payable.

The most common mistake that QB newbies make in Bill Pay looks like this: The business owner receives a bill from a vendor and enters it into "Enter Bills" in the vendor module of the software. They then pay the bill by writing a check directly from the Check Register. This sounds innocent enough, but it causes a huge problem.

The issue is that the Check Register is in no way connected to the bill that was entered, so it doesn't post the payment toward that bill, and Accounts Payable continues to show the bill unpaid. As a result, the business checking account balance gets smaller, but the Accounts Payable balance doesn't. This generates a FUBAR'd Balance Sheet report showing inflated amounts of debt.

To post a bill's payment toward its balance, you must pay the bill through the same module that you entered it into in the first place.

Do it right or don't do it at all!

1. When you receive a bill from a vendor, enter it in Bill Pay's "Enter Bills."

2. Pay the bill through Bill Pay's "Bill Payment"—not through your Check Register.

Using this method is like freakin' magic, the bill is marked paid on the client side, the amount is posted in the check registers and funds are subtracted from your bank balance/credit card, and the amount paid is posted to the Accounts Payable balance.

RECEIVING PAYMENTS FOR DUPLICATE INCOME
(CHAPTER 7)

Our seventh QuickBooks SNAFU closely parallels number 6, which will hopefully make it easier to understand. In number 6, we talked about the Bill Pay module in QuickBooks, a.k.a. Accounts Payable. Now we'll cover the Receiving Payments module, a.k.a. Accounts Receivable.

Bill Pay = Accounts Payable
Received Payments = Accounts Receivable

Here's the most common mistake made by newbies receiving payments: The business owner creates an invoice in the "Create Invoices" section, and when the customer pays that invoice the business owner enters the deposit directly into the Check Register. This may seem innocuous, but it's sure trouble.

The problem, once again, is that the Check Register is not connected to the invoice that was created, so it doesn't post the payment to Accounts Receivable. Instead, the funds go straight to the bank, and it looks like the invoice was never paid.

Your customer's invoice remains unpaid in your Accounts Receivable, which is on your Balance Sheet. Are you beginning to see how important number 2 is? Your financial report will show your business is owed money that it isn't actually owed and your brain says "I know that's paid. Why is this still showing unpaid?" You've got other things to do so do this right the first time.

> *Don't screw up posting payments you receive! Deposits entered in the Check Register don't post toward the customer's account. That only happens in "Receive Payment."*

Be an Ace

1. Create an Invoice for product or services rendered in "Create Invoices."

2. When you receive the payment for the invoice, be sure it's recorded through "Receive Payment."

3. When you click "Receive Payment" and select the customer, the open invoice should be listed there, and you'll check it off in the highlighted area and click "Enter." The funds now post either to the bank account you specified in preferences, OR they go to "Undeposited Funds."

4. You must also go to "Record Deposit" to make sure the post is completed. Like freakin' magic, the payment is posted to your customer's account, the funds are deposited, and the balance is removed from Accounts Receivable.

> *"Undeposited Funds" can be a really scary hiccup.*
> *It's vital that you understand how to handle this correctly.*

Dida Clifton

"Undeposited Funds" is an account that is part of the QuickBooks accounting software. It's not something you created and you can't remove or delete it. Think of it like this: Imagine you've received several payments from customers throughout the week in the form of a check or cash and you placed those payments on your desk. They are waiting to be deposited to the bank. In this scenario, your desk is the undeposited funds account.

When you create your deposit slip and take those to the bank, then they become "deposited funds." You'll need to do the same in your bookkeeping software.

1. Post the payment through "Receive Payments."

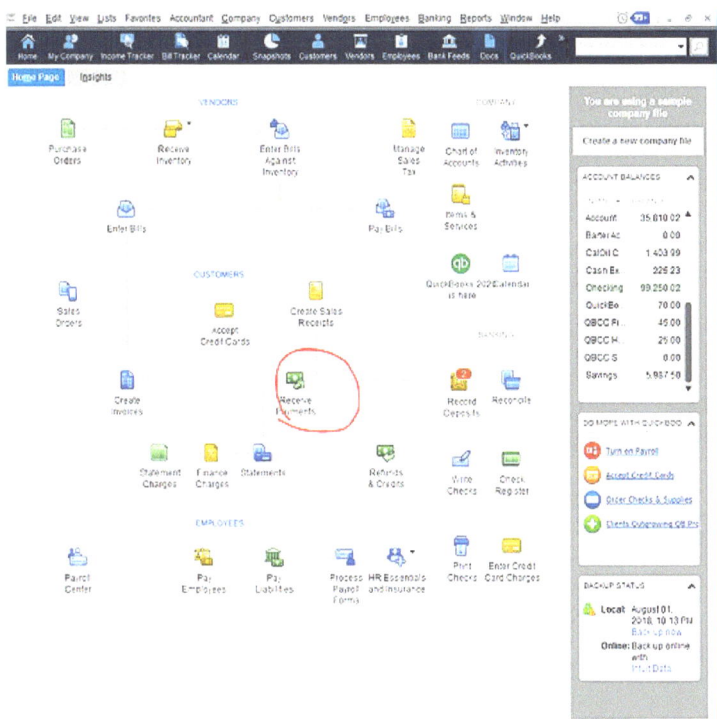

2. Record the deposit.

3. Select items from "Undeposited Funds" to deposit.

4. Create your deposit slip.
   It needs to match exactly what was deposited.

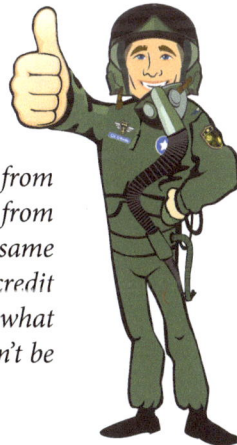

> **Reality Check:** *Credit card payments from your clients and end of day batches from your merchant service are treated the same way. Your daily deposits from the credit card processor need to match exactly what was deposited that day. If not, you won't be able to reconcile the bank account.*

DON'T BE THE FNG: VENDORS VS. EMPLOYEES
(CHAPTER 8)

Woo-hoo! You made it to number 8 of the top ten most common QuickBooks SNAFUs!

The eighth most common do-it-yourself business bookkeeping error is paying a person as a vendor when they should be classified as an employee. Also, too often vendors are set up incorrectly in QuickBooks. This mistake may cost you money. Sooner or later it will cost you time.

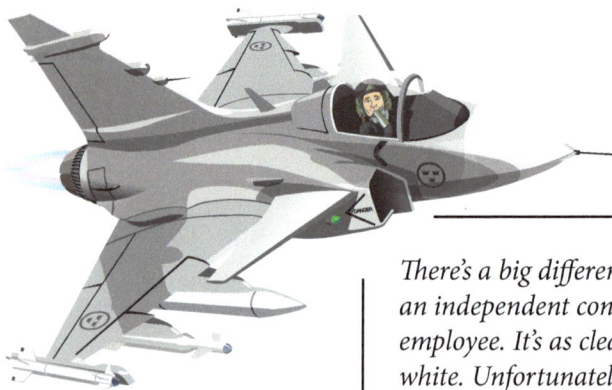

> *There's a big difference between an independent contractor and an employee. It's as clear as black and white. Unfortunately, many business owners see nothing but gray area.*

The answer is as simple as two little words: A duck. If it walks like a duck, and it quacks like a duck, it's a duck. In other words, if the position requires the employee to be directed as to how, when, where and with what to do the job, then get quacking; he or she is a W-2 employee. However, if the job will be done independently, then it's likely that a 1099 is the way to go.

Is your duck a vendor?

An employee is "on the payroll," and The Taxman knows them by their W-2. They may be part time, full time, or temporary and may be paid on either an hourly or salary basis.

A vendor doing work for you is called an independent contractor or a 1099 vendor. They are considered self-employed. Vendors are associated with tax forms W-9 and 1099. The number of hours they work for you can vary drastically. So can the way their pay is calculated.

It's become increasingly common over the past ten years for businesses to hire workers under the tax status of independent contractor. Some employers hire these 1099ers because it can ultimately be cheaper and lower risk, and it's definitely a better fit for the commitment-phobic. However, if it comes down to it, the IRS ultimately determines whether you have assigned the correct worker status. If it's decided later that you were incorrect in your choice, you'll be paying back payroll taxes, penalties, and fees dating back to the beginning of that relationship.

SETTING UP VENDORS CORRECTLY FOR THE TAXMAN

When it's time to pay your Vendor, don't forget to set them up correctly in your QuickBooks. If you pay someone more than $600 in a year and they are not a corporation or an employee, then they get a 1099 at the end of the year for their tax return. It's the law.

In order for QuickBooks to do the calculation for you and print the 1099, you'll need to make sure you set them up properly as a vendor. Collecting a W-9 from all vendors will assure that you have all the correct information. You'll need to enter their full mailing address, their social security number or federal tax ID (EIN), and check the box indicating a 1099 vendor.

Here's another trend: Many independent contractors don't want a 1099; they prefer cash pay, leaving no paper trail for The Taxman. If you do this, and many do, that expense is not deductible to your company and becomes your income.

Airman, do you really want to pay someone else's taxes?

CHECK YOUR 6:
RECONCILE OR REGRET
(CHAPTER 9)

> I hope by this point you've learned something new from all this. If not, you either know it all or you're not paying attention.

The ninth most common do-it-yourself bookkeeping error is not reconciling accounts. Many newbies don't even know what that means. I wish I were joking.

Each and every month you must compare what your bank and credit card statements list to what you've entered in QuickBooks. Yes. Every month. This monthly reconciliation for each account confirms that everything is in its place, that it's all correct, and ensures there are no surprises that sneak up on your 6.

It's easy to be fooled into believing that a special app or syncing capabilities are all you need. Not true. In order for your business to have complete and accurate financials, you need to make sure that everything the bank says happened really did happen. Banks do make errors.

> *Your bank account can sync with your QuickBooks ALL DAY LONG, but Airman, that bird don't fly! You must do MORE to accurately reconcile.*

TheOfficeSquad's pro bookkeepers find large amounts of inaccurate charges when reconciling for our client businesses. We find clients that have been double-charged. We spot amounts transposed and notice extra zeros. What should have been a $280 purchase cleared the bank as $2,800. One zero. Big difference. You're thinking, "I would definitely notice that." This client didn't and it wasn't discovered until three months after it happened. Must be nice to have balances in your accounts large enough that you don't notice those things, right? Let's get you there!

When tax time arrives and you present your P&L and Balance Sheet to your tax preparer, the only way to know if those numbers are accurate is through reconciling. You can be sure of your numbers and see that everything is entered into the correct QuickBooks account in less than an hour a month. That one hour will save you 10, and could also save you thousands of dollars.

DO THE IMPOSSIBLE: ENTER EVERY DAMN THING
(CHAPTER 10)

Drum roll please…

Number 10 of The Top 10 QuickBooks errors is simply not entering everything.

As the owner of a small business, your main focus is gaining revenue for the sake of survival. And if you are responsible for the bookkeeping as well, your focus remains on gaining revenue. You create the invoices, you get them to the customer, and you collect the money. This way of being is basically vital to your business, but too often important bookkeeping steps are neglected.

> *Reality Check: There just never seems to be enough time and the bookkeeping doesn't demand that you do it. It's a silent but serious side of the mission and fight for success. Done at regular intervals, with accuracy and precision, it can become a habit that leads to a smooth landing every month.*

Sometimes it's little things that were overlooked along the way, or items that were simply entered incorrectly. At tax time this leaves you scrambling to find help, remember or gather details, and complete tasks that should have been done a long time ago. Running your business and the tax deadlines don't wait, which is stressful enough without having to cram an entire year (or two) of bookkeeping into three months or less.

> *QuickBooks is your friend, Civvy. You can always count on it, unless it can't count on you. If you need assistance, your mission is to reach out for a wingman!*

Everything goes in QuickBooks.

Every loan.

Every payment.

Every invoice.

Every large purchase over $600, such as equipment, tools, trailers, and automobiles.

Every dollar that you as a business owner put into the business.

Every dollar that you as the business owner took out.

Set it up correctly, manage it throughout each month, and you'll be just fine.

We'll be your wingman!
V/R,
Dida and Col. QB
TheOfficeSquad

THE GLOSS:
A GLOSSARY OF JARGON, SLANG & ACRONYMS
(QUICKBOOKS & AIR FORCE)

Accounts payable – *noun.* "**uh-kOUnts pAY-uh-buhl**" A current liability account showing the amount a company owes for purchases made on a credit card.

Accounts receivable – *noun.* "**uh-kOUnts ri-sEE-vuh-buhl**" An asset resulting from goods sold or services rendered, for which payment is expected.

Airman – *noun.* "**AIR-muhn**" A pilot or member of an aircraft's crew, especially in the Air Force.

Assets – *noun.* "**A-sets**" Resources owned by a company with a worth that can be expressed in dollars. Includes objects, cash, investments, and accounts receivable.

Balance sheet – *noun.* "**bAl-uhns sheet**" An important financial report that includes assets, liabilities, and stockholders' equity at a point in time. Also called Statement of Financial Position.

[On the] barber pole – *adjective.* "**[AWn THuh] bAHR-buhr pOHl**" Going top airspeed. This references the red and white striped needle on airspeed indicators that marks the maximum allowable speed. See full-throttle.

Basic training – *noun.* **"bAY-sik trAY-ning"** Initial training period for new military personnel involving intense physical activity and behavioral discipline.

Box nasty – *noun.* **"bAHks nAs-tee"** A sandwich & snack meal in a cardboard box handed out for flights.

Cash flow report – *noun.* **"kAsh flOH rEE-pohrt"** An important financial report that covers sources and uses of cash for a certain period. Also known as the Statement of Cash Flows.

CFO – *noun.* **"sEE-Ef-OH"** Chief Financial Officer. A common title for the top-ranking financial person in a corporation.

Charlie foxtrot – *noun.* **"chAHR-lee fAHks-traht"** A clean alternative for clusterf*ck. Used to describe a complex and disastrously disorganized or mishandled situation. "That office is a total Charlie Foxtrot when she's out of town."

Chart of accounts – *noun.* **"chAHRt uhv uh-kOUnts"** Vital part of QuickBooks that lists each of your assets, liabilities, income, and expense accounts.

Check register – *noun.* **"chEk rEj-uh-stuhr"** Your business' "checkbook." Includes deposits, checks written, bank charges, bank credits, and the resulting balance.

Check your six – *verb.* **"chEk yOR sIks"** Look behind you. Six o'clock is behind you. (Twelve o'clock is in front.)

Civvies – *noun.* **"sIv-eez"** Civilians. Also, Normies or Joedies.

Classified information – *noun.* **"klAs-uh-fied in-fuhr-mAY-shuhn"** Official information that requires protection in the interest of national security. Unclassified information does not require secrecy.

COA – *noun.* **"sEE-OH-AY"** Chart of Accounts. A listing of the user's accounts that are available in QuickBooks including balance sheet accounts and income statement accounts.

Dida Clifton

Depreciation – *noun.* **"di-pree-shee-AY-shuhn"** The result of a formula determining the cost of a tangible asset over its lifetime, factoring its decline in value.

Draw – *noun.* **"drAW"** The withdrawal of business assets for personal use by the business owner.

Don't fly/won't fly – *verb.* **"dOHnt flIE/wOHnt flIE"** Phrase indicating that something is dysfunctional, ineffective, or unpassable. "That bird don't fly."

Double entry accounting – *noun.* **"dUHb-uhl En-tree uh-kOUn-ting"** A time-tested accounting system where every transaction is recorded in at least two accounts.

Embrace the suck – *verb.* **"im-brAYs THuh sUHk"** Slang used among junior enlisted acknowledging that they have little say in undesirable decisions. It's effectively advice that one should not worry themselves over things they cannot control.

Equity – *noun.* **"Ek-wuh-tee"** The difference between a business' assets and its liabilities.

Fangs out – *verb.* **"fAngz OWt"** To get aggressive; to go for the kill. "I saw that auditor and my fangs came out."

Fighter pilot breakfast – *noun.* **"fIE-tuhr pIE-luht breK-fuss"** A Coke, a smoke and a puke. You civvies should eat real meals.

Flight – *noun.* **"flIEt"** A unit of the U.S. Air Force below a squadron; a group of similar beings or objects flying through the air together.

Flight path – *noun.* **"flIEt pAth"** The actual planned course of an aircraft.

Flying Ace – *noun.* **"flIE-ing AYs"** A military aviator credited with shooting down several enemy aircraft during combat.

FNG – *noun.* **"Ef-En-jEE"** Freakin' new guy. Too often doesn't have the info you need. A viable alternative to "NUB."

FM/PFM – *noun.* **"Ef-Em / pEE-Ef-Em"** Freakin' magic/pure freakin' magic. Used to describe something too complex for you to understand the workings of. "QuickBooks Desktop is PFM, we're lucky it's around!" Also used for a technical problem that solves itself.

FUBAR – *adjective.* **"fOO-bAHr"** F@#$ed Up Beyond All Recognition. Don't let your books get like this. If they're already like this, it's time to call in TheOfficeSquad's Special Ops team.

Full-throttle – *adverb.* **"fUl thrAHt-l"** Doing something at full speed or with great intensity.

Go down in flames – *verb.* **"gOH dOUn In flAYmz"** To fail spectacularly, ending suddenly and completely.

Grease(d) [a landing] – *verb, phrase.* **"grEEst uh lAn-ding"** To skillfully perform a very smooth landing of an aircraft, without bumps. "You should've seen how I greased that one!"

Goat rope – *noun.* **"gOHt rOHp"** An unbelievably messed up situation. "It was a real goat rope out there today!" Also see FUBAR and Charlie Foxtrot.

HQ – *noun.* **"AYch-kyOO"** Headquarters, home base, a.k.a. mother. This can refer to an aircraft carrier or to the Pentagon, depending on context.

ID 10 T Problem – *noun.* **"eye-Dee ten tee prAHb-lem"** A problem that is created by an "idiot."

Intel – *noun.* **"in-tEl."** Information of military value. Military intelligence.

Keep the blue side up – *phrase.* **"kEEp THuh blOO sIEd UHp"** An aviation saying that is a way of wishing someone well, referring to the sky vs. the ground. If the blue side is down and not up, something is really, really wrong.

Liabilities – *noun.* **"lie-uh-bIl-uh-teez"** Amounts a company owes to lenders and suppliers. Often have the word "payable" in the account title.

Dida Clifton

MIA – *adjective.* **"em-ie-AY"** Acronym for "missing in action;" describes something or someone mysteriously and unexpectedly lost.

Mission – *noun.* **"mIsh-uhn"** An operation carried out by military aircraft. Also, an important assignment carried out for commercial purposes with goals and purpose.

NUB – *noun.* **"nOOb"** New Useless Bastard, New Boy, Newbie.

P&L – *noun.* **"pEE uhnd El"** Profit and Loss Statement, a.k.a. the Revenue/Income Statement. One of the main financial reports showing the profitability of a company during a certain period of time.

PICNIC – *noun.* **"pɪk,nɪk"** An acronym meaning "Problem in Chair, Not in Computer." Used by technical support personnel to indicate user ignorance. "Their supposed network issue is a PICNIC problem."

Pop tart – *noun.* **"pAHp tAHRt"** Airmen whose technical career schools are six weeks or less in duration.

Queep – *noun.* **"kWEEp"** A task or duty that is completely useless and ultimately unrelated to your primary job. Often assigned by superiors who assume you have nothing else important to do. "I have a lot of queep to do before I go home."

Reconcile – *verb.* **"rEk-uhn-sie-uhl"** A process confirming that amounts listed on a bank statement are consistent with the balance in the company's account.

Secret squirrel stuff – *noun.* **"sEE-kruht skwUHR-ruhl stUHf"** Material classified as top secret or other special compartmentalized information.

SKT – *noun.* **"es kay tee"** Specialty Knowledge Test.

SNAFU – *noun.* **"sna-fOO"** Situation Normal All F@#$ed Up. Used when it's all gone awry.

SNAFU-interceptor – *noun.* **"sna-fOO in-tuhr-sEp-tuhr"** A business process or method that prevents a financial SNAFU scenario from forming. (see: SNAFU)

Spirit mission – *noun.* **"spIR-uht mIsh-uhn"** A good-natured act, commonly in the form of a prank or a reacquisition of a person or thing, to show pride for a group of individuals. Usually harmless.

Stand by – *verb.* **"stand bie"** A communications radio expression meaning "please wait."

Squad – *noun.* **"skwad"** A small group engaged in a common effort or occupation.

SWAG – *noun.* **"swag"** Scientific Wild-Ass Guess. A rough estimate made by an expert in the field, based on experience and intuition.

The Taxman – *proper noun.* **"Thee tAks-man"** Slang for the IRS, a.k.a. the U.S. Internal Revenue Service.

TLAR – *affirmative.* **"tee el a R"** That Looks About Right.

Unsafe airspace – *noun.* **"uhn-sAYf AIR-spays"** An area within which activities dangerous to the flight of an aircraft may exist.

V/R – Very Respectfully (closing salutation).

Wingman – *noun.* **"wingmuhn"** "Wingman" is the plane flying beside and slightly behind the lead plane in an aircraft formation. A wingman is a pilot who supports another in a potentially dangerous flying environment. TheOfficeSquad is ready when you need us!

Woo-hoo! – *interjection, informal.* **"woo-hoo"** Expression of excitement and delight. " I tried to yell woo-hoo when I reached Mach 2, but I couldn't actually utter a word."

Dida Clifton

THE PHONETIC OR NATO ALPHABET

The International Civil Aviation Organization (ICAO) assigned codewords acrophonically to the letters of the English alphabet, so that critical combinations of letters and numbers are most likely to be pronounced and understood by those who exchange voice messages by radio or telephone, regardless of language differences or the quality of the communication channel.

A: ALFA	J: JULIETT	S: SIERRA
B: BRAVO	K: KILO	T: TANGO
C: CHARLIE	L: LIMA	U: UNIFORM
D: DELTA	M: MIKE	V: VICTOR
E: ECHO	N: NOVEMBER	W: WHISKEY
F: FOXTROT	O: OSCAR	X: XRAY
G: GOLF	P: PAPA	Y: YANKEE
H: HOTEL	Q: QUEBEC	Z: ZULU
I: INDIA	R: ROMEO	

1: WUN	5: FIFE	9: NIN-ER
2: TOO	6: SIX	0: ZEE-RO
3: TREE	7: SEV-EN	
4: FOW-ER	8: AIT	

NOTES

Dida Clifton

_____

_____

_____

_____

_____

_____

_____

_____

_____

_____

_____

_____

_____

_____

_____

_____

_____

_____

_____

_____

_____

_____

_____

Dida Clifton

www.ingramcontent.com/pod-product-compliance
Lightning Source LLC
LaVergne TN
LVHW010036070426
835513LV00005B/122